PENGUIN BOOKS

QUOTABLE NEW YORK

William Cole is a veteran anthologist. He has
lived in the heart of New York City for most of
his life.

QUOTABLE

NEW YORK

A LITERARY COMPANION

Edited by William Cole

PENGUIN BOOKS

PENGUIN BOOKS
Published by the Penguin Group
Penguin Books USA Inc., 375 Hudson Street,
New York, New York 10014, U.S.A.
Penguin Books Ltd, 27 Wrights Lane,
London W8 5TZ, England
Penguin Books Australia Ltd, Ringwood,
Victoria, Australia
Penguin Books Canada Ltd, 10 Alcorn Avenue,
Toronto, Ontario, Canada M4V 3B2
Penguin Books (N.Z.) Ltd, 182–190 Wairau Road,
Auckland 10, New Zealand

Penguin Books Ltd, Registered Offices: Harmondsworth,
Middlesex, England

First published in the United States of America as *New York:
A Literary Companion* by Pushcart Press 1992
Published in Penguin Books 1993

1 3 5 7 9 10 8 6 4 2

ISBN 0-916366-59-6 (hc.)
ISBN 0 14 01.7631 4 (pbk.)

Printed in the United States of America
Designed by Mary Kornblum/Hudson Studio

Is the True New Yorker different from everybody else? The True New Yorker will say no. But, he's different; he knows tricks and shortcuts, things to do and things not to do, to make life easier. In *Bech Is Back* John Updike, a one-time True New Yorker, hits the nail on the nose with " . . . he had the true New Yorker's secret belief that people living anywhere else had to be, in some sense, kidding." Exactly. And, as a True New Yorker, I've assembled a bouquet of epiphanies that will help distinguish the True New Yorker from Those Other People.

The True New Yorker knows—

. . . that pressing the CLOSE DOOR button in an office building elevator won't get you off the first floor any faster.

. . . never to speak to strangers on a bus. But True New Yorkers will vie with one another to make change for tourists, particularly foreign ones.

. . . never to look at a street nut—a shouter or talker-to-himself. If he catches your eye, he might shout and rave at *you*.

. . . that renting a car will *always* come to much more than you had estimated. The same with moving men.

. . . that no True New Yorker ever uttered "Avenue of the Americas." Nor does he say "F. D. R. Drive." It's the East River Drive.

. . . that the "DON'T WALK" usually blinks from ten to fourteen times, and that it is safe to saunter across during the first five, or scamper the next. Note: a few exceptions on Fifth Avenue blink only five.

. . . that the best way to get a taxi midtown—during rush hours, or in the rain, or on New Year's Eve, is to enter a large hotel and emerge again on the taxi queue.

. . . never to talk with strangers on the street, except when viewing accidents or arguments, or in cases of natural phenomena such as hailstorms or blizzards.

. . . that it is wisest to walk in the middle of the street after dark in deserted neighborhoods. Also, nobody will ever try to mug a crazy, so it might be wise to rave and wave your arms about.

. . . to unhitch that velvet rope at the bank—or step over it—instead of winding sheepishly through the maze.

. . . that doubling the sales tax on your restaurant check will give an adequate tip.

. . . to say "House-ton" not "Hews-ton" Street. And "Henri Bendel" is pronounced without a trace of French.

. . . that the chances are one in ten that only half of the subway door will slide open.

. . . that in any large record store there is always one surprisingly young clerk who knows the entire stock. This is certainly not true of book stores.

. . . to buy twenty tokens at a time to avoid long lines at subway booths.

. . . that a watch isn't really a necessity; and the time can always be seen through the windows of banks, barber shops, and dry cleaners.

. . . never to take a taxi or a bus crosstown on a parade day.

. . . how to get anywhere in Manhattan by the judicious use of bus transfers.

. . . there's only a 50/50 chance that the cabbie will know his destination or how to get there. There's a 25/75 chance that he won't understand English.

. . . that there is one restaurant in Chinatown that is the *best*. It is his personal discovery, and he will never reveal the name to a chance aquaintance.

. . . to check that there's no deposit of water on the bus seat he's about to sit on. Rainy weather means frequent wet seats.

. . . that if he locates the woman's room in a public building, by some conspiracy of plumbing the men's will be somewhere in the vicinity.

. . . that a single woman, at night, standing against a building, is not necessarily waiting for any specific person.

. . . not to buy anything from a camera or gift shop in a high rent area, especially if there's a "going out of business" sign.

. . . that it is a confusing business to try to figure which buses stop at which stops going up Madison or down Fifth.

∴ . . to exit from the front door of buses. The back door is often a struggle to open. Some buses bear a yellow strip at the top of the rear doors; pushing these open is easy.

. . . to pay no attention to the timetables posted at bus stops. "Schedule of approximate arrival times" is approximate, indeed.

. . . that he can usually locate a bathroom midtown on the mezzanine floor of a large hotel. These serve the ballroom or "function rooms."

. . . that the Chinese waiter won't understand him. Always ask for the headwaiter; he *might*.

. . . that taxis at night can usually be found outside expensive restaurants. Or in the morning on uptown avenues, when most people are headed south.

. . . that anyone walking a dog is necessarily a native of that neighborhood, and as such is a good bet to give reliable directions.

. . . that it takes a minute to walk a north/south block, five minutes for a crosstown.

. . . that New Yorkers stand *on* line, not *in* line.

. . . that it is just as effective to shout "Tax!" as "Taxi!"

. . . that when a True New Yorker refers to "The Hamptons," the phrase does not embrace Hampton Bays. And probably not Westhampton, either.

. . . that doormen, superintendents, and the maintainence crew of co-op buildings become a hundred percent nicer and more cooperative in the first three weeks of December.

. . . that just because an area is south of Houston, it ain't necessarily SoHo.

. . . that it will do no good to ask your busboy for anything more than bread and water. Few speak any English.

. . . that some people refer to that department store as "Bloomies." Others think that rather vulgar.

. . . that a reference to "The Met" means the opera, "The Metropolitan" the museum.

. . . that if he must engage a gypsy cab or cruising limousine, he must get a price from the driver while his hand is still on the door handle.

. . . the peculiar thrill of finding himself on an unfamiliar city street. "Hey! I've never been on this block before!"

. . . not to take the top newspaper on the pile; he pulls out the third or fourth under. He also carries something to clean the *New York Times* off his hands.

. . . that delicatessens and cleaners in the vicinity of large hotels will always be madly overpriced.

. . . that the number six bus, on its run down Seventh and Broadway to the Battery, carries the most tourists. They climb aboard with guide books, and it sounds like a moving Tower of Babel.

. . . that when someone works "downtown" the reference is to Wall Street.

. . . that the True New Yorker will always look at a celebrity, but will pretend to be totally unimpressed.

. . . that the Outerbridge Crossing, from remote Staten Island to remote New Jersey, is not named for its remoteness, but for Eugenius Outerbridge, the first Port Authority boss.

. . . that a reference to "The Village" always refers to the old, once Bohemian West Village. The East Village is always referred to as such.

. . . that when you want coffee with milk, you ask for "regular." For black, you say "Black."

. . . that nowhere in the City of New York can you turn right on red.

. . . to profess puzzlement when visitors to the City talk about the hurry and frenzy. The True New Yorker says, "What hurry? What frenzy?"

If you still don't understand New York, read on. Hundreds of opinions follow. After reading this little collection, you will know all you need to know about New York, or almost all. Or at least a bit.

WILLIAM ROSSA COLE

NEW YORK

Here is a great house and there a ginshop, or a tailor's or a grocery. Such is the character of New York. The old families which were an aristocracy have given way. The new ones are coming forward on the strength of wealth suddenly acquired and which in all probability will be as suddenly lost. Adventurers dash in for the spoils and the thousand and one bloodsuckers who are found in the haunts of a corrupt city. I should never be anxious to live in such a city.

CHARLES FRANCIS ADAMS (1834)

Vaudevillian Eddie Foy remarked, in discussing the engineering feat of the Brooklyn Bridge, 'All that trouble just to get to Brooklyn.'

JOEY ADAMS

There is no city in the world that has a greater influence. . . . All over this continent it is imitated, even where it is said to be feared. Men say New York is a warning rather than an example, and then proceed to make it an example. Outside America, New York is America, and its skyscraper a symbol of the spirit of America. It is not only the largest city in the world, it is the greatest and most powerful that is not a capitol of a nation.

THOMAS ADAMS (1931)

A brilliant morning with a slight haze. The first discernable thing after passing the Ambrose Lightship is the Brooklyn gasometer. This is on the right. Next, on the left, the Statue of Liberty, a big girl who is obviously going to have a baby. The Birth of a Nation, I suppose.

JAMES AGATE (1938)

I . . . wonder what it is in the New York air that enables me to sit up till all hours of the night in an atmosphere which in London would make a horse dizzy, but here merely clears the brain.

JAMES AGATE

New York is the place of casual acquaintances who become your Great-and-Good-Friends in *Time*.

NELSON ALGREN

The intellectual life is why I'm a New Yorker. It's why I stay here. I spend my summers in Europe, and if they ask me if I'm an American, I say, "No, I'm a New Yorker." I don't know about everyone else, but for me that's a positive statement.

ALEXANDER ALLAND, JR.

There is no question there is an unseen world; the question is, how far is it from midtown, and how late is it open?

WOODY ALLEN

I think you know that when an American stays away from New York too long something happens to him. Perhaps he becomes a little provincial, a little dead and afraid.

SHERWOOD ANDERSON

When you ride the subway twice a day, it's difficult to think of the immortal soul.

ANONYMOUS

New Yorkers are inclined to assume it will never rain and certainly not on New Yorkers.

BROOKS ATKINSON

New York is the only city in the world where you can get deliberately run down on the sidewalk by a pedestrian.

RUSSELL BAKER

The only real advantage of New York is that all its inhabitants ascend to heaven right after their deaths, having served their full term in hell right on Manhattan Island.

BARNARD COLLEGE BULLETIN

The muck heaves and palpitates. It is multidirectional and has a mayor.

DONALD BARTHELME

New York is the Mecca of everyone in the world who has an independent will and a conception of the century he lives in. New York is the gateway to the 48 freedoms—which may not be enough, but which are unquestionably better than the seven devils left behind. New York means all this and earns its greatness, but by a paradox of equal magnitude, it fails in all the practical modernity it supposedly stands for. As a city to live in, New York is a squatter's camp.

JACQUES BARZUN (1954)

I miss New York and its fairy-like towers
With Liberty's torch high in the air
I'd give all of California's damn flowers
For the sight of Washington Square.

JESSIE TARBOX BEALS

After twenty annual visits, I am still surprised each time I see this giant asparagus bed of alabaster and rose and green skyscrapers.

CECIL BEATON

Babylon-on-the-Make.

LUCIUS BEEBE

New York is my Lourdes, where I go for spiritual refreshment. . . . a place where you're least likely to be bitten by a wild goat.

BRENDAN BEHAN

I am not afraid to admit that New York is the greatest city on the face of God's earth. You only have to look at it, from the air, from the river, from Father Duffy's statue. New York is easily recognizable as the greatest city in the world, view it any way and every way—back, belly and sides.

BRENDAN BEHAN

I think New York is not the cultural center of America, but the business and administrative center of American culture.

SAUL BELLOW

I regard it as a curiosity; I don't let myself get caught in the wheels.

LUDWIG BEMELMANS

For most visitors to Manhattan, both foreign and domestic, New York is the Shrine of the Good Time. This is only natural, for outsiders come to New York for the sole purpose of having a good time, and it is for their New York hosts to provide it. The visiting Englishman, or the visiting Californian, is convinced that New York is made up of millions of gay pixies, flitting about constantly in a sophisticated manner in search of a new thrill. "I don't see how you stand it," they often say to the native New Yorker who has been sitting up past his bedtime for a week in an attempt to tire his guest out.

ROBERT BENCHLEY

Each man reads his own meaning into New York.

MEYER BERGER

Everybody ought to have a lower East Side in their life.

IRVING BERLIN

A great many people go after success simply for the shiny prizes it brings . . . And nowhere is it pursued more ardently than in the city of New York.

STEPHEN BIRMINGHAM

21

East Side, West Side, all around the town,
The tots sang "Ring-a-rosie," "London Bridge is falling
down";
Boys and girls together, me and Mamie O'Rorke,
Tripped the light fantastic on the sidewalks of New
York.

    JAMES W. BLAKE (1894)

City of dreadful height.

    JAMES BONE

Bunting of all nationalities and of no nationality was
flaunting over the streets. Poles of liberty accentuated
the 'Rights of Man.' Bands of Music preceded proces-
sions of a dozen boys, bearing flags and tattered tar-
gets. Irish was spoken in the wharves, German in the
saloons, French in the restaurants. But the chiefest fea-
ture in this polyglot city was its boyhood. A boy in
heart, but a man, and a very shrewd one, in head!

    DION BOUCICAULT (1889)

New York waiters, probably the surliest in the Western world . . . are better images of their city than the journalistic favorite—the taxi driver . . . The majority of them give the impression of being men who have been drafted into the job during a period of martial law and are only waiting to get back to a really congenial occupation such as slum demolition or debt collecting.

ALAN BRIEN

One of the few charms that Manhattan has for me is its nearly complete freedom from one of the most annoying of American habits: impertinent curiosity about other people's affairs.

SIR DENIS BROGAN

Any fool can stand upon a hill in the country and be aware that grass is up and trees have begun to bud; but in the city spring is served a la carte rather than in heaping portions. Back on my farm lie heavy woods, yet none of these trees appeals to me so deeply as a scrubby sapling which grew in the back yard of my house in New York—when a tree digs its roots down among water pipes and gas mains and thrusts its way up through dust and cinders, that's something. I sometimes think that never blooms a tulip quite so red as that which shows its head in a Park Avenue flower bed between the traffic. We Manhattan nature lovers love her best because we know so little about her.

HEYWOOD BROUN

If you live in New York, even if you're Catholic, you're Jewish.

LENNY BRUCE

New Yorkers are nice about giving you street directions; in fact they seem quite proud of knowing where they are themselves.

KATHERINE BRUSH

As for New York City, it is a place apart. There is not its match in any other country in the world.

PEARL S. BUCK

When can a city be said to be dying? For one thing, when its past far outshines its present and overwhelms the future, and New York is at that point. The giants have gone, along with the good days and easy nights.

HERB CAEN (1976)

I love short trips to New York; to me it's the finest three-day town on earth.

JAMES CAMERON

I am just coming out of five years of night, and this orgy of violent lights gives me for the first time the impression of a new continent. An enormous, 50-foot high Camel billboard: a GI with his mouth wide open blows enormous puffs of *real* smoke. So much bad taste hardly seems imaginable.

ALBERT CAMUS (1946)

Sometimes, from beyond the skyscrapers, the cry of a tugboat finds you in your insomnia, and you remember that this desert of iron and cement is an island.

ALBERT CAMUS

The Solomon R. Guggenheim Museum . . . is a war between architecture and painting in which both come out badly maimed.

JOHN CANADAY

New York is the only real city-city.

TRUMAN CAPOTE

For weeks afterward I philandered in New York, dining, wining, lunching, dancing and revelling in the luxuries of a city untouched by war. The shops were a delight and not expensive. Luxury abounded. Everyone gave grand galas in my honour. . . . I was fête ad absurdum, and almost ad nauseam. Never have I felt so well, never so triumphant.

SIR HENRY (CHIPS) CHANNON (August, 1945)

The present in New York is so powerful that the past is lost.

JOHN JAY CHAPMAN (1909)

I don't suppose there was a day, an hour, when the middle class got their marching orders, but toward the end of the 1940s the middle class began to move . . . the rich of the city were getting richer and the friable middle ground where we stood was vanishing.

JOHN CHEEVER

When I had a look at the lights of Broadway by night, I said to my American friends: "What a glorious garden of wonders this would be, to any who was lucky enough to be unable to read."

G. K. CHESTERTON

The shrine to which the lords of capitalism commute in cattle cars.

JOHN CIARDI

The food in the city's most celebrated dining salons, with one or perhaps two exceptions, is neither predictably elegant nor superb. More often it is predictably commonplace.

CRAIG CLAIBORNE

When you are away from old Broadway you are only camping out.

GEORGE M. COHAN

New York is a great city to live in if you can afford to get out of it.

WILLIAM ROSSA COLE

Never let the poor and destitute emigrant stop at New York—it will be his ruin.

CALVIN COLTON (1832)

New York, New York! It's a wonderful town! The west side of the island was rich in facades not unlike the possibilities of a fairy princess with syphilis.

RICHARD CONDON

That sinister Stonehenge of economic man, Rockefeller Center.

CYRIL CONNOLLY

I always knew children were anti-social. But the children of the West Side—they're savage.

MARC CONNELLY

New York is the biggest collection of villages in the world.

ALISTAIR COOKE

It seemed almost intolerably shining, secure and well-dressed, as though it was continually going to gay parties while London had to stay home and do the housework.

NOEL COWARD

First New York was a sort of provincial capital, bigger and richer than Manchester or Marseilles, but not much different in its essential spirit. Then, after the war, it became one among half a dozen world cities. Today it has the appearance of standing alone, as the center of culture in the part of the world that still tries to be civilized.

MALCOLM COWLEY (1939)

What separates New York from the rest of the country (and let's forget the lordly Hudson) is—in the field of entertainment—quantity, and of course the chauvinists among us would like to add, quality—with some justification.

JUDITH CRIST

A bulger of a place it is. The number of the ships beat me all hollow, and looked for all the world like a big clearing in the West, with the dead trees all standing..

DAVY CROCKETT (1835)

Even though I've been coming to the States for many years, I don't write about New York. The city alarms me.

ROBERTSON DAVIES

She has become a wicked and wild bitch in her old age has Manhattan, but there is still no sensation in the world quite like walking her sidewalks. Great surges of energy sweep all around you; the air fizzes like champagne, while always there is a nervous edge of fear and whispered distant promises of sudden violence.

TOM DAVIES (1979)

Any man who can afford a hall bedroom and a gas-stove in New York City is better off than he would be as the owner of one hundred and sixty acres on the prairie, or in one of these small so-called cities.

RICHARD HARDING DAVIS (1892)

There is something in the New York air that makes sleep useless.

SIMONE DE BEAUVOIR

There is one quarter, commonly called the Five Points, which in respect of filth and wretchedness, may be safely backed against Seven Dials, or any other part of famed St. Giles . . . these narrow ways, diverging to the right and left, and reeking everywhere with dirt and filth. Such lives as are led here, bear the same fruits here as elsewhere. The coarse and bloated faces at the doors, have counterparts at home, and all the wide world over. Debauchery has made the very houses prematurely old. See how the rotten beams are tumbling down, and how the patched and broken windows seem to scowl dimly, like eyes that have been hurt in drunken frays. Many of those pigs live here. Do they ever wonder why their masters walk upright in lieu of going on all-fours? and why they talk instead of grunting?

CHARLES DICKENS (1842)

It is often said that New York is a city for only the rich and the very poor. It is less often said that New York is also, at least for those of us who came there from somewhere else, a city for only the very young.

JOAN DIDION

I mean that I was in love with the city, the way you love the first person who ever touches you.

JOAN DIDION

When I first saw New York I was 20, and it was summertime, and I got off a DC-7 at the old Idlewild temporary terminal in a new dress which had seemed very smart in Sacramento but seemed less smart already.

JOAN DIDION

The thing that impressed me then as now about New York . . . was the sharp, and at the same time immense, contrast it showed between the dull and the shrewd, the strong and the weak, the rich and the poor, the wise and the ignorant . . . the strong, or those who ultimately dominated, were so very strong, and the weak so very, very weak—and so very, very many.

THEODORE DREISER

Nearly all th' most foolish people in th' country an manny ivth' wisest goes to Noo York. Th' wise people ar-re there because th' foolish wint first. That's th' way th' wise men make a livin'.

FINLEY PETER DUNNE (1901)

New York is at once cosmopolitan and parochial, a compendium of sentimental certainties. It is in fact the most sentimental of the world's great cities—in its self-congratulation a kind of San Francisco of the East.

JOHN GREGORY DUNNE

Then at the street intersection I had the shock of see-ing a black policeman directing traffic—and there were white drivers who obeyed his signals as though it was the most natural thing in the world . . . This really was Harlem.

RALPH ELLISON (on arriving from the South)

New York is a sucked orange.

RALPH WALDO EMERSON

New York is the greatest city in the world for lunch . . . That's the gregarious time. And when that first martini hits the liver like a silver bullet, there is a sigh of contentment that can be heard in Dubuque.

WILLIAM EMERSON JR.

I'm going to show you the real New York—witty, smart, and international—like any metropolis. Tell me this—where in Europe can you find old Hungary, old Russia, old France, old Italy? In Europe you're trying to copy America, you're almost American. But here you'll find Europeans who immigrated a hundred years ago— and we haven't spoiled them. Oh, Gio! You must see why I love New York. Because the whole world's in New York. . . .

ORIANA FALLACI

Over the great bridge, with sunlight through the girders making a constant flicker upon the moving cars, with the city rising up across the river in white heaps and sugar lumps all built with a wish out of non-olfactory money. The city seen from the Queensboro Bridge is always the city seen for the first time, in its first wild promise of all the mystery and the beauty in the world.

F. SCOTT FITZGERALD

I carry the place around the world in my heart but sometimes I try to shake it off in my dreams.

F. SCOTT FITZGERALD

I have withdrawal symptoms at picnics on Long Island.

JOE FLAHERTY

New York is large, glamorous, easy-going, kindly and incurious—but above all it is a crucible—because it is large enough to be incurious.

FORD MADOX FORD

New York is a different country. Maybe it ought to have a separate government. Everybody thinks differently, acts differently—they just don't know what the hell the rest of the United States is.

HENRY FORD

(A definition of hell): "New York City with all the escape hatches closed."

JAMES R. FRAKES

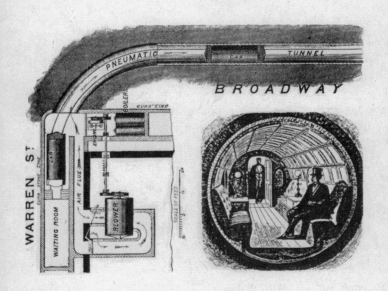

An island in the Atlantic.
WALDO FRANK

A street of ham and aches.
HY GARDNER

New York is a good spot to stop away from.
CROSBIE GARSTIN

New York . . . that unnatural city where every one is an exile, none more so than the American.
CHARLOTTE PERKINS GILMAN

New York remains what it has always been: a city of ebb and flow, a city of constant shifts of population and economics, a city of virtually no rest. It is harsh, dirty, and dangerous, it is whimsical and fanciful, it is beautiful and soaring—it is not one or another of these things but all of them, all at once, and to fail to accept this paradox is to deny the reality of city existence.
PAUL GOLDBERGER

New York is an arrogant city; it has always wanted to be all things to all people, and a surprising amount of the time it has succeeded. It has always been a city of commerce, and the values of commerce have tended to supercede other values. There is no pretense here of excessive gentility, and the rush was always to the new, the large, the prosperous, the fashionable.

    PAUL GOLDBERGER

I remember how often some of us walked out of the darkness of the Lower East Side and into the brilliant sunlight of Washington Square.

    HARRY GOLDEN

It was early June and New York was already a ghost town. The rich had departed at the first sign of a Puerto Rican with a transistor. Politicians hung in to turn on a few fire hydrants and pose with some wet Third Worlders before taking off on junkets that kept them away until Labor Day.

    HEYWOOD GOULD

E.C.T

A VIEW OF THE CITY HALL, NEW YORK,
During the Drawing of the Lottery.

The foundation stone of this noble building was laid on the 26th of September, 1803, during the Mayoralty of Edward Livingston, Esq. and at a time when the Yellow Fever prevailed in the City. It was finished in 1812, and the expense exclusive of the furniture amounted to half a million of Dollars. The first story, including the portico, is of the Ionic, the second of the Corinthian, the attic of the Fancy, and the Cupola of the Composite orders.

IT IS 3:30 IN THE MORNING AND I AM THE
ONLY ONE IN THIS SUBWAY STATION AND I'M
SCARED

GRAFFITO (1970)

I couldn't sleep for my first two weeks here. I remember the energy and the hostility. The chaos. I enjoy it.
The anonymity, even. You may have a career and be
somewhat visible in your field and yet have the sense
of a private life.

NANCY GRAVES

New York is the greatest city in the world—especially
for my people. Where else, in this grand and glorious
land of ours, can I get on a subway, sit in any part of
the train I please, get off at any station above 110th
Street, and know I'll be welcome?

DICK GREGORY

It (Brooklynese) was a dialect of confusions . . . these
linguistic confusions were the reflection of deeper confusions. They mirrored the inverted psychology of the
natives who called their heroes 'Bums.'

FRANCES GRIFFITHS

It is late. (Joan) Miro and all of us, walk briefly toward Third Avenue. It has become even chillier. Miro breathes in the air. "Ah, what vitamins! This city is a tonic! This city is a doctor!"

JOHN GRUEN

New York is hard, cynical, ruthless, even beyond other cities. From their early repression its children emerge sophisticated, both stunted and overdeveloped, perverted, premature, forced by the artificiality of their environment.

ERNEST GRUENING

New York City, the incomparable, the brillant star city of cities, the forty-ninth state, a law unto itself, the Cyclopean Paradox, the inferno with no out-of-bounds, the supreme expression of both the miseries and the splendors of contemporary civilization, the Macedonia of the United States. It meets the most severe test that may be applied to definition of a metropolis—it stays up all night. But also it becomes a small town when it rains.

JOHN GUNTHER

The city of right angles and tough, damaged people.

PETE HAMILL

Mothers born on relief have their babies on relief. Nothingness, truly, seems to be the condition of these New York people. . . . They are nomads going from one rooming house to another, looking for a toilet that functions.

ELIZABETH HARDWICK

This city is the size of a country but it has been operated like a candy store.

JOEL HARNET

New York is notoriously the largest and least-loved of any of our great cities. Why should it be loved as a city? It is never the same city for a dozen years altogether. A man born in New York forty years ago finds nothing, absolutely nothing, of the New York he knew. If he chances to stumble upon a few old houses not yet leveled, he is fortunate. But the landmarks, the objects which marked the city to him, as a city, are gone.

HARPER'S (1856)

The lusts of the flesh can be gratified anywhere; it is not this sort of license that distinguishes New York. It is rather, a lust of the total ego for recognition, even for eminence. More than elsewhere, everybody here wants to be somebody.

SYDNEY J. HARRIS

The only credential the city asked was the boldness to dream. For those who did, it unlocked its gates and its treasures, not caring who they were or where they came from.

MOSS HART

'The filthiest, most crime-ridden spot in the world,' one fashionable New York lady called it. Helen (Hayes) instantly blazed out in its defense. 'But can't you realize,' she demanded, 'that our city is so big it's got to have the most of everything? And by the very same token, it's got more that's good than any place I know.'

HELEN HAYES and ANITA LOOS

There's a trace of the erotic about the way we Manhattanites regard Brooklyn. The Bronx may supply guffaws. Queens may make us yawn, and Harlem start us jiving but Brooklyn touches our very libidos. Among the innumerable graffiti that have been scrawled on Brooklyn Bridge by strolling couples, there ought to be one, spelled out in lights, that reads: "Manhattan loves Brooklyn."

HELEN HAYES and ANITA LOOS

A city where wise guys peddle gold bricks to each other and Truth, crushed down to earth, rises again as phoney as a glass eye.

BEN HECHT

This is New York, a combat zone, and everyone has to have an angle or they're not allowed over the bridges or through the tunnels. Let them have their angles, it's what they live for. You've got better things to worry about, like making sure the people that actually matter don't try any funny stuff.

CYNTHIA HEIMEL

It's a town you come to for a short time.

ERNEST HEMINGWAY

47

There is more sophistication and less sense in New York than anywhere else on the globe.

DON HEROLD

You come to New York to find the ambiance that will evoke your best. You do not necessarily know precisely what that might be, but you come to New York to discover it.

DR. JAMES HILLMAN

The city is a zoo for people. It's a cement zoo for the crazy. It's the same thing as when you take monkeys out of the jungle and put them in cages. They sit there and masturbate. The cities are places where people sit and masturbate.

CHICKEN HIRSCH

I'd rather listen to a flute
In Gotham, than a band in Butte.

SAMUEL HOFFENSTEIN

Overturn, overturn, overturn! is the maxim of New York. The very bones of our ancestors are not permitted to lie quiet a quarter of a century, and one generation of men seems studious to remove all relics of those who preceded them.

PHILIP HONE (1845)

Melting pot Harlem—Harlem of honey and chocolate and caramel and rum and vinegar and lemon and lime and gall. Dusky dream Harlem rumbling into a nightmare tunnel where the subway from the Bronx keeps right on downtown.

LANGSTON HUGHES

. . . the Hilton is layed out with a competence that would make a computer blush.

ADA LOUISE HUXTABLE

It wasn't until I got to New York that I became Kansan. Everyone there kept reminding me that they were Jewish or Irish, or whatever, so I kept reminding them that I was midwestern. Before I knew it, I actually began to brag about being from Kansas! I discovered that I had something a bit unique, but it was the nature of New York that forced me to claim my past.

WILLIAM INGE

It's a fickle town, a tough town. They getcha, boy. They don't let you escape with minor scratches and bruises. They put scars on you here.

REGGIE JACKSON

New York is appalling, fantastically charmless and elaborately dire.

HENRY JAMES

It is altogether an extraordinary growing, swarming, glittering, pushing, chattering, good-natured, cosmopolitan place, and perhaps in some ways the best imitation of Paris that can be found (with a great originality of its own).

HENRY JAMES

(The Village) is a lotus land in which gaiety is synthetic, poverty is fashionable and real, hilarity is forced, honor is infrequent, purpose is pie-eyed, ambition is asleep, and art is merely an excuse for everything.

RIAN JAMES (1930)

A beautiful catastrophe.

CHARLES E. JEANNERET

New York, like London, seems to be a cloacina of all the depravities of human nature.

THOMAS JEFFERSON

On the island of Manhate, and in its environs there may well be four or five hundred men of different sects and nations; the Director General told me there were men of eighteen different languages.

FR. JOGUES, S. J. (1646)

In New York people don't go to the theatre—they go to see hits.

LOUIS JOURDAN

Brooklyn Heights itself is a window on the port. Here, where the perspective is fixed by the towers of Manhattan and the hills of New Jersey and Staten Island, the channels running between seem fingers of the world ocean. Here one can easily embrace the suggestion, which Whitman felt so easily, that the whole American world opens out from here, north and west.

ALFRED KAZIN

Cut off as I am, it is inevitable that I should sometimes feel like a shadow walking in a shadowy world. When this happens I ask to be taken to New York City. Always I return home weary but I have the comforting certainty that mankind is real and I myself am not a dream.

HELEN KELLER

The faces in New York remind me of people who played a game and lost.

MURRAY KEMPTON

Whenever spring comes to New York I can't stand the suggestions of the land that come blowing over the river from New Jersey and I've got to go. So I went.

JACK KEROUAC

I don't like the life here. There is no greenery. It would make a stone sick.

NIKITA S. KRUSHCHEV

The world is grand, awfully big and astonishingly beautiful, frequently thrilling. But I love New York.

DOROTHY KILGALLEN

America's hardened artery.

MARK KELLY

A neighborhood is where, when you go out of it, you get beat up.

MURRAY KEMPTON

New York is a quiet sort of place, where nobody much knows anybody else, and the people work hard or pretend to, and go to bed with a glass of hot milk, having previously hotted up a hamburger in an immaculate five-thousand-dollar kitchen.

LORD KINROSS

No one as yet had approached the management of New York in a proper spirit; that is to say, regarding it as the shiftless outcome of squalid barbarism and reckless extravagance. No one is likely to do so, because reflections on the long narrow pig-trough are construed as malevolent attacks against the spirit and majesty of the American people, and lead to angry comparisons.

RUDYARD KIPLING

To start with, there's the alien accent. "Tree" is the number between two and four. "Jeintz" is the name of the New York professional football team. A "fit" is a bottle measuring seven ounces less than a quart. This exotic tongue has no relationship to any of the approved languages at the United Nations, and is only slightly less difficult to master than Urdu.

FLETCHER KNEBEL

Water, water, everywhere
Atlantic and Pacific
But New York City's got them beat
Our aqua is terrific!

MAYOR EDWARD KOCH

Mass is said in 23 different languages in this city.

MAYOR EDWARD KOCH

As a city, New York moves in the forefront of today's great trend of great cities toward neurosis. She is confused, self-pitying, helpless and dependent.

JOHN LARDNER

A hundred times have I thought New York is a catastrophe, and fifty times: It is a beautiful catastrophe.

LE CORBUSIER

. . . no dumping ground, no sewer, no vault contains more filth or in greater variety than does the air in certain parts of New York City during the long season of drought. . . . No barrier can shut it out, no social distinction can save us from it; no domestic cleanliness, no private sanitary measures can substitute a pure atmosphere for a foul one.

LESLIE'S WEEKLY, (1881)

In New York it's not whether you win or lose—it's how you lay the blame.

FRAN LEBOWITZ

When you leave New York, you are astonished at how clean the rest of the world is. Clean is not enough.

FRAN LEBOWITZ

Traffic signals in New York are just rough guidelines.

DAVID LETTERMAN

New York now leads the world's great cities in the number of people around whom you shouldn't make a sudden move.

DAVID LETTERMAN

New York is, after all, a place of business; it is not constructed to be lived in.

WYNDHAM LEWIS

Not only is New York the nation's melting pot, it is also the casserole, the chafing dish and the charcoal grill.

MAYOR JOHN V. LINDSAY

Robinson Crusoe, the self-sufficient man, could not have lived in New York City.

WALTER LIPPMANN

New York attracts the most talented people in the world in the arts and professions. It also attracts them in other fields. Even the bums are talented.

EDMUND LOVE

There are only about four hundred people in New York society.

WARD MCALLISTER

It is said that New York is the wickedest city in the country. It is the largest, and vice thrives in crowded communities . . . Yet, if it is the wickedest city, it is also the best on the Continent. If it contains thousands of the worst men and women in our land, it contains also thousands of the brightest and the best of Christians. In point of morality, it will compare favorably with any city in the world . . . Being the great centre of wealth and culture, New York is also the centre of everything that is good and beautiful in life.

JAMES D. MCCABE JR. (1882)

Ah! some love Paris,
And some Purdue.
But love is an archer with a low I.Q.
A bold, bad bowman, and innocent of pity.
So I'm in love with
New York City.

PHYLLIS MCGINLEY

I come from New York, where if you fall down, someone will pick you up by your wallet.

AL MCGUIRE

A car is useless in New York, essential everywhere else.
The same with good manners.

MIGNON MCLAUGHLIN

The Americans are justly very proud of it, and its res-
idents passionately attached to it . . . a young New
Yorker, who had been in Europe for more than a year,
was in the same sleigh with me. "There goes the old
city!" said he in his enthusiasm, as we entered Broadway; "I could almost jump out and hug a lamp-post!"

ALEXANDER MACKAY (1849)

Part of the oncoming demise (of New York during its terrible fiscal crisis) is that none of us can simply believe it. We were always the best and the strongest of cities, and our people were vital to the teeth. Knock them down eight times and they would get up with that look in the eye which suggests the fight has barely begun.

NORMAN MAILER

Teenagers in the ghetto see the hell caught by their parents struggling to get somewhere. They make up their own minds that they would rather be like the hustlers whom they see dressed "sharp" and flashing money. So the ghetto youth becomes attracted to the hustler worlds of dope, thievery, prostitution, general crime and immorality.

MALCOLM X

Most of the people living in New York have come here from the farm to try to make enough money to go back to the farm.

DON MARQUIS

A person who speaks good English in New York sounds like a foreigner.

JACKIE MASON

If, in New York, you arrive late for an appointment, say, "I took a taxi."

ANDRE MAUROIS

. . . the greatest city of the modern world, with more money in it than all Europe and more clowns and harlots than all Asia, and yet it has no more charm than a circus lot or a second-rate hotel.

H. L. MENCKEN

It seems to me that you are better off, as a writer and as an American, in a small town than you'd be in New York. I thoroughly detest New York, though I have to go there very often. . . . Have you ever noticed that no American writer of any consequence lives in Manhattan? Dreiser tried it (after many years in the Bronx), but finally moved to California.

H. L. MENCKEN

Under barrel-vaulted ceilings and among the vibrations of trains, in a spot 12.6 miles from the Atlantic Ocean, 28 feet above sea level and 22 feet below 42nd Street, at the epicenter of the metropolis that annually devours $1.5 billion worth of seafood, the most in the nation—stands Grand Central Terminal's celebrated seafood restaurant, the Oyster Bar.

DAVID MICHAELIS

When it's three o'clock in New York, it's still 1938 in London.

BETTE MIDLER

My one thought is to get out of New York, to experience something genuinely American.

HENRY MILLER

New York has a trip-hammer vitality which drives you insane with restlessness if you have no inner stabilizer.

HENRY MILLER

He speaks English with the flawless imperfection of a New Yorker.

GILBERT MILLSTEIN

Roaming the streets of New York, we encountered many examples of this delightful quality of New Yorkers, forever on their toes, violently, restlessly involving themselves in the slightest situation brought to their attention, always posing alternatives, always ready with an answer or an argument.

JESSICA MITFORD

In Rome I am weighted down by a lack of momentum, the inertia of a spent civilization. In New York I feel plugged into a strong alternating current of hope and despair.

TED MORGAN

New York, the nation's thyroid gland.

CHRISTOPHER MORLEY

New York is Babylon: Brooklyn is the truly Holy City. New York is the city of envy, office work, and hustle; Brooklyn is the region of homes and happiness. . . . There is no hope for New Yorkers, for they glory in their skyscraping sins; but in Brooklyn there is the wisdom of the lowly.

CHRISTOPHER MORLEY (1917)

And so in the end I was left, like so many voyagers before me, trapped by the great port. I loathed it like a lover. The questions it asked I resented; the answers it gave I mistrusted; the delight I felt to be unfair. Damn you, New York! Damn the bright sweep of your spaces, and the ungainly poetry of your names! A curse on all your archipelago, and those rough fresh winds off your bay—which, catching me like an embrace as I stepped out of the helicopter, so often ravished my spirits and made my heart sing.

JAMES MORRIS

And it was to this city, whenever I went home, that I always knew I must return, for it was mistress of one's wildest hopes, protector of one's deepest privacies. It was half insane with its noise, violence, and decay, but it gave one the tender security of fulfillment. On winter afternoons, from my office, there were sunsets across Manhattan when the smog itself shimmered and glowed . . . Despite its difficulties, which become more obvious all the time, one was constantly put to the test by this city, which finally came down to its people; no other place in America had quite such people, and they would not allow you to go stale; in the end they were its triumph and its reward.

WILLIE MORRIS

The city is not a concrete jungle, it is a human zoo.

DESMOND MORRIS

Unfortunately there are still people in other areas who regard New York City not as a part of the United States, but as a sort of excrescence fastened to our Eastern shore and peopled by the less venturesome waves of foreigners who failed to go West to the genuine American frontier.

ROBERT MOSES

I venture to predict that long after the public has wearied of Frank Lloyd Wright's inverted oatmeal dish and silo with their awkward cantilevering, their jaundiced skin and ingenious spiral ramp leading down past the abstractions which mirror the tortured maladjustments of our time, the Metropolitan will still wear well.

ROBERT MOSES

The skyscrapers began to rise again, frailly massive, elegantly utilitarian, images in their grace, audacity and inconclusiveness, of the whole character of the people who produces them.

MALCOLM MUGGERIDGE

He who touches the soil of Manhattan and the pavement of New York, touches, whether he knows it or not, Walt Whitman.

LEWIS MUMFORD

Thousands of people lived under the shadow of the elevated, with the smoke of the old-fashioned locomotives puffing into their windows, with the clank and rattle causing them to shout in daily conversation to overcome the roar outside. The obliviousness to low sounds, the indifference to cacophony which makes the ideal radio listener of present-day America, was part of the original acquisition of Manhattan in these decades.

LEWIS MUMFORD (1934)

I remember not being surprised or overwhelmed by New York. I found it the way I expected it to be; a kind of immense vertical mess (Edmund Wilson used to call it real estate gone mad) set upon a square horizontal order.

NICOLAS NABOKOV

Most human beings are driven to seek security and comfort. But there is another group that can only thrive on change and the unexpected of New York.

CATHLEEN NESBIT

Vulgar of manner, overfed,
Overdressed and underbred;
Heartless, Godless, hell's delight,
Rude by day and lewd by night . . .
Crazed with avarice, lust and rum,
New York, thy name's delirium.

BYRON RUFUS NEWTON (1906)

New York City is made up of five boroughs, four of which—Brooklyn, Queens, Richmond, the Bronx—compose like crinkled lily pads about the basking trout of Manhattan.

NEW YORK PANORAMA (FEDERAL WRITERS'
PROJECT OF THE WPA)

The thing I can't tell is whether cab drivers yield to each other out of fear or respect.

NEW YORK POLICEMAN

I miss the animal bouyancy in New York, and the animal vitality. I did not mind that it had no meaning and no depth.

ANAIS NIN

A New Yorker is a person with an almost inordinate interest in mental health, which is only natural considering how much of that it takes to live here.

NEW YORK TIMES

Poets have celebrated the wit and sonority of the names of American towns, but to our way of thinking they are not a patch on the telephone exchanges of New York. We linger over the rippling liquefaction of "SUsquehanna," the sturdiness of "MOnument," the liveliness of "SPring." We dote on forthright "CAnal" and sing of sweet "LOrraine." These are names to dial and conjure with. And what of our rich legacy from an OLder CIvilization—stirring names like "TRafalgar," "OXford," "WHitehall," "CHelsea," and "REgent"? Is this great tradition to be curtailed on behalf of intercity dialing?

NEW YORK, (1961)

Any city gets what it admires, will pay for, and, ultimately deserves. Even when we had Penn Station, we couldn't afford to keep it clean. We want and deserve tin-can architecture in a tin-horn culture. And we will probably be judged not by the monuments we build but by those we have destroyed.

NEW YORK TIMES (1963)

I tell you, there were times when as Mayor, I truly wanted to jump. You would look out over the city from someplace high above, and you would say to yourself, "Good Jesus, it's too much for me."

WILLIAM O'DWYER

A man who strolls in Hyde Park after nightfall may possibly find himself in the police court next morning. (It would largely depend on what kind of lady he met, and what sort of adventures attract him). But the man who strolled in Central Park after nightfall would almost certainly find himself in the morgue.

COLLINSON OWEN (1929)

It'll be a great place if they ever finish it.

O. HENRY

"Been in the city long?" inquired the New Yorker, getting ready for the exact tip against the waiter's coming with large change from the bill.

"Me?" said the man from Topaz City. "Four days. Never in Topaz City, was you?"

"I!" said the New Yorker. "I was never farther west than Eighth Avenue. I had a brother who died on Ninth, but I met the cortege at Eighth . . . I cannot say that I am familiar with the West."

O. HENRY

In dress, habits, manners, provincialism, routine and narrowness, he acquired that charming insolence, that irritating completeness, that sophisticated crassness, that overbalanced poise that makes the Manhattan gentleman so delightfully small in his greatness.

O. HENRY

I can't even enjoy a blade of grass unless I know there's a subway handy.

FRANK O'HARA

I've been in New York for ten years, and the only people who are nice to us turn out to be Moonies.

P. J. O'ROURKE

When you visit Gotham, you should ride out the Fifth Avenue, as far as the distributing reservoir, near Forty-third Street, I believe. The prospect from the walk around the reservoir is particularly beautiful. You can see from this elevation, the north reservoir at Yorkville; the whole city to the Battery; with a large portion of the harbor, and long reaches of the Hudson and East rivers. Perhaps even a finer view, however, is to be obtained from the summit of the white, light-house-looking shot-tower which stands on the East river, at Fifty-fifth Street, or thereabouts.

EDGAR ALLAN POE

I have been roaming far and wide over this island of Manhatta. . . . The city is thronged with strangers, and everything wears an aspect of intense life. Business has experienced a thorough revival, and "all goes merry as a marriage bell." Notwithstanding the Croton water, or "the Crot'n," as the Gothamites have it, the streets are, with rare exception, insufferably dirty. The exceptions are to be found in Bond Street, Waverly Place, and some others of the upper, more retired, and more fashionable quarters. . . .

EDGAR ALLAN POE

A crowd pagan as ever imperial Rome was, eager, careless with an animal vigor unlike that of any European crowd that I ever looked at.

EZRA POUND

The crisis in human dignity. . . . I've been spat on, vomited on, pushed and shoved, delayed three hours in a fire, and wound up on a D train which became an F train in midflight.

HAROLD M. PROSHANSKY

New York as I recollect it, had a much sweeter smell in those days, that is, the late eighties. There was no disgusting gasoline to poison the air, and when one walked out early in the morning there was a floating breath of wood-smoke that vaguely recalled villages in Wales and Normandy.

ERNEST RHYS (1931)

One day there was four innocent people shot. That's the best shooting ever done in this town. Hard to find four innocent people in New York.

WILL ROGERS

You know, the more they knock New York, the bigger it gets.

WILL ROGERS

There are certainly numberless women of fashion who consider it perfectly natural to go miles down Fifth Avenue, or Madison Avenue, yet for whom a voyage of half a dozen blocks to east or west would be an adventure, almost a dangerous impairment of good breeding.

JULES ROMAINS

That's the New York thing, isn't it. People who seem absolutely crazy going around telling you how crazy they used to be before they had therapy.

JUDITH ROSSNER

The shape of Manhattan island was like that of a sole, with its head at Harlem, and its tail at the Castle garden: the backbone being represented by Broadway, and the continuous line of ships fringing the wharves along the East River and the Hudson River respectively, figuring the lateral small bones of the fish.

G. A. SALA

He probably passed on . . . of an overdose of garlic, the way all New York barbers eventually do.

J. D. SALINGER

There's no room for amateurs, even in crossing streets.

GEORGE SEGAL

. . . the upper East Side of Manhattan. This is the province of Let's Pretend located in the State of Anomie.

GAIL SHEEHY

New York—It's overpriced, it's dark, it's insular, it has absolutely no idea of what's going on in the rest of the country. The only thing it cares about is what it creates itself, and most of that is an illusion. I think that its days as a cultural force are numbered. New York is a horrible place.

IAN SHOALES

There are two million interesting people in New York and only seventy-eight in Los Angeles.

NEIL SIMON

The chief complaint I have about living in the Big Town is the necessity now and then of showing it off to my kinfolks or other unreasonable citizens from the Edgar Guest country.

H. ALLEN SMITH

Manhattan is a narrow island off the coast of New Jersey devoted to the pursuit of lunch.

RAYMOND SOKOLOV

New York, home of the vivisectors of the mind, and of the mentally vivisected still to be reassembled, of those who live intact, habitually wondering about their states of sanity, and home of those whose minds have been dead, bearing the scars of resurrection. . . .

MURIEL SPARK

In the streets of New York between seven and nine in the morning you will see the slow procession of dog and owner proceeding from street to tree to hydrant to trash-basket. They are apartment dogs. They are taken out twice a day, and, while it is a cliché, it is truly amazing how owner and dog resemble each other. They grow to walk alike, have the same set of head.

JOHN STEINBECK

As we drew near New York I was at first amused, and then somewhat staggered, by the cautious and grisly tales that went round. You would have thought we were to land upon a cannibal island. You must speak to no one in the streets, as they would not leave 'til you were rooked and beaten. You must enter a hotel lobby with military precautions; for the least you had to apprehend was to awake the next morning without money and baggage, or necessary raiment, a lone forked radish in a bed; and if the worst befell, you would instantly and mysteriously disappear from the ranks of mankind.

ROBERT LOUIS STEVENSON

I like to walk around Manhattan, catching glimpses of its wild life, the pigeons and cats and girls.

REX STOUT

New York has more hermits than will be found in all the forests, mountains and deserts of the United States.

SIMEON STRUNSKY

When I leave it I never dare look back lest I turn into a pillar of salt and the conductor throws me over his left shoulder for good luck.

FRANK SULLIVAN

The pneumatic noisemaker is becoming the emblematic Sound of New York, the way the bells of Big Ben are the Sound of London.

HORACE SUTTON

. . . New York, where 250 people die each day, and where the living dash for empty apartments . . . Where on page 29 of this morning's newspaper are pictures of the dead; on page 31 are pictures of the engaged; on page 1 are pictures of those who are running the world, enjoying the lush years before they land back on page 29.

GAY TALESE

Under this Sun people can't sit still, people can't ruminate over the dinner, dawdle in their studies and be lazy and tranquil—they must keep moving, rush from one activity to another, jump out of sleep and to their business, have lean eager faces—I want to dash into the street now. At home after breakfast I want to read my paper leisurely and then get to my books and work. . . . Yesterday some rain began to fall. I felt a leaden cap taken off my brain pan and began to speak calmly and reasonably, & not wish to quit my place.

W. M. THACKERAY (1855)

Speaking of New York as a traveler, I have two faults to find with it. In the first place, there is nothing to see; and, in the second place, there is no mode of getting about to see anything.

ANTHONY TROLLOPE

Situated on an island which I think it will one day cover, it rises like Venice from the sea, and like that fairest of cities in the days of her glory, receives into its lap tribute of all the riches of the earth.

FRANCES TROLLOPE (1827)

You cannot imagine what an infatuation church-going has become in New York. Youths and young misses, young gentlemen and ladies, the middle-aged and the old, all swarm to church, morning, noon and night, every Sunday.

MARK TWAIN (1867)

. . . An office block, possibly made of pre-stressed celery.

KENNETH TYNAN

Hemingway described literary New York as a bottle full of tapeworms trying to feed on each other.

JOHN UPDIKE

. . . the true New Yorker's secret belief that people living anywhere else had to be, in some sense, kidding.

JOHN UPDIKE

Skyscraper national park.

KURT VONNEGUT

I'd rather be a lampost in New York than Mayor of Chicago.

MAYOR JAMES J. WALKER

An idea, a song, a discovery, an invention, may be born anywhere. But if it is to be communicated, if it is to be tested and compared and appreciated, then someone has always to carry it to the city.

MAX WAYS

And suddenly as I looked back at the skyscrapers of lower New York a queer fancy sprang into my head. They reminded me quite irresistibly of piled-up packing-cases outside a warehouse. I was amazed I had not seen the resemblance before. I could really have believed for a moment that that was what they were, and that presently out of these would come the real thing, palaces and noble places, free, high circumstances, and space and leisure, light and fine living for the sons of men.

H. G. WELLS

To Europe she was America, to America she was the gateway of the earth. But to tell the story of New York would be to write a social history of the world.

H. G. WELLS

New York City is a great apartment hotel in which everyone lives and no one is at home.

GLENWAY WESCOTT

If you are confused ask somebody. New Yorkers are very helpful. However, the first person you ask will give you the wrong answer. So ask loudly enough that others will overhear and make corrections. New Yorkers love to correct each other.

GEORGE WELLER

It can destroy an individual, or it can fulfill him, depending a good deal on luck. No one should come to New York to live unless he is willing to be lucky.

E. B. WHITE

To an outlander a stay in New York can be and often is a series of small embarrassments and discomforts and disappointments: not understanding the waiter, not being able to distinguish between a sucker joint and a friendly saloon, riding the wrong subway, being slapped by a bus driver for asking an innocent question, enduring sleepless nights when the street noises fill the bedroom.

E. B. WHITE

Taxis roll faster than they did ten years ago—and they were rolling fast then. Hackmen used to drive with verve; now they sometimes seem to drive with desperation, toward the ultimate tip. On the Westside Highway, approaching the city, the motorist is swept along in a trance—a sort of fever of inescapable motion, goaded from behind, hemmed in on either side, a mere chip in a millrace.

E. B. WHITE

The beautiful city, the city of hurried and sparkling
waters! the city of spires and masts!
The City nested in bays! my city!
The city of such women, I am mad with them! I will
return after death to be with them!
The city of such young men, I swear I cannot live
happy without I often go talk, walk, eat, drink, sleep
with them!

WALT WHITMAN

More and more too, the old name absorbs into me
Mannahatta, 'the place encircled by many swift tides
and sparkling waters.' How fit a name for America's
great democratic island city! The word itself, how
beautiful! how aboriginal! how it seems to rise with tall
spires, glistening in sunshine, with such New World atmosphere, vista and action!

WALT WHITMAN

The Senegalese street vendors are different from other vendors. They are polite, for one thing; even the police who arrest them note this. They speak little English, but they speak it with a soft French accent. They sell everything, but they are partial to gold trinkets and watches. Like other vendors, they buy from the jobbers.

They do not hawk their wares; they just stand silently behind their trays of goods. If they do address a customer, it is with a whispered question. Gold watches? Gold watches? Their serenity is disarming.

WILLIAM H. WHYTE

The city has always been a source of creativity. In the suburbs, there's no human interaction, no chance meetings. That's the central function of a city: to bring people together, face to face, *mano a mano*. They talk about what a rat race it is, but they love it. That's why the city will survive forever.

WILLIAM H. WHYTE

I was the walking epitome of fur*shirr* meets yo'ass. On my first day in New York I went to school dressed like a typical California kid: I wore tie-up yoga pants and a Hawaiian shirt, and I kept stepping in dog shit with my thongs.

ROBIN WILLIAMS

One is glad to come back to the gray New York air, the cold faces, the colorless buildings.

EDMUND WILSON

A little strip of an island with a row of well-fed folks up and down the middle, and a lot of hungry folks on each side.

HARRY LEON WILSON

The Sheridan Apartment House stands in the heart of New York's Bohemian and artistic quarter. If you threw a brick from any of its windows, you would be certain to brain some rising interior decorator, some Vorticist sculptor or a writer of revolutionary *vers libre*.

P. G. WODEHOUSE

One belongs to New York instantly, one belongs to it as much in five minutes as in five years.

THOMAS WOLFE

One hears the hoarse notes of the great ships in the river, and one remembers suddenly the princely girdle of proud, potent tides that bind the city, and suddenly New York blazes like a magnificent jewel in its fit setting of sea, and earth, and stars.

THOMAS WOLFE

There is no place like it, no place with an atom of its glory, pride, and exultancy. It lays its hand upon a man's bowels; he grows drunk with ecstasy; he grows young and full of glory, he feels that he can never die.

THOMAS WOLFE

At night . . . the streets become rhythmical perspectives of glowing dotted lines, reflections hung upon them in the streets as the wistaria hangs its violet racemes on its trellis. The buildings are shimmering verticality, a gossamer veil, a festive scene-prop hanging there against the black sky to dazzle, entertain, amaze.

FRANK LLOYD WRIGHT

They come from all over the country to New York. The executive's wife decided they will move to New York. She says, 'John, you're the boss now. I've been doing the laundry and raising the kids all my life. It's time we enjoyed opening nights in New York.' So the company packs up and moves.

WILLIAM ZEKENDORF

Cities always define themselves in relation to New York. In the early 1980s, Indianapolis had a slogan that said, "Move over New York, apple is our middle name."

STEVEN ZEITLIN

Who the hell looks up, in this town? Who has time?

DAVID ZICKERMAN